Mega Max and Lugs

Rocket Man

by David Walke

Mr Max is a big man.
He lives in a big city –
Mega City.

Mr Max has a secret.
When he eats garlic
crisps he turns into Mega
Max – Superhero!

Mr Max is a teacher at Mega City High School.
Mr Lugg works at City High too. Out of school they
are Mega Max and Lugs. Mega Max keeps the city
safe. Lugs is always at his side …

The sun was high over Mega City. Mr Max was in the staffroom. He picked up the phone.
"I'm going to Mega City Labs today, Lugs. Do you want to come?" he said.

"Yes, sir," said Lugs.
"Good! Get the van," said Mr Max.

Lugs has a van. It looks like the school van. But when he pushes a button it turns into the Mega Van. The Mega Van can do clever stuff.

Lugs took the school van across the city. When they got to Mega City Labs they got out. Mr Max looked around.

"Look at that," he said. On a pad next to the lab was a big silver rocket.

A man came out of the lab.

"Hello, Smith," said Mr Max.

"Good morning, Mr Max," said the man.

"We're going to send a rocket up soon. Come into the lab."

Mr Max and Lugs went in.

It was dark in the lab. There were lots of screens and computers. A map of the planets was on a big screen.
"Where is the rocket going?" asked Lugs.
"To the Sun," said Smith.

"The computers track the rocket. We can see it on these big screens," said Smith.
"This red button fires the rocket."
"What does the green button do?" asked Mr Max.
"It's for our new Cosmic Cola," said Smith. "Have a cup."

Lugs got two cups of
Cosmic Cola.
Mr Max took a cup.
"Oops!" he said.
He dropped it.

The Cosmic Cola went
all over the computer.
"Look out! Fire!" yelled
Smith.
The computer was on fire.

"Help! Call 999! Fire!" yelled Smith.
"There's no time," said Mr Max. He ripped the computer desk open. It was full of flames. The smoke got in his eyes.

Mr Max took off his coat.
"Look out, sir!" yelled Lugs.
"I'm OK," said Mr Max. He stuffed his coat up into the desk. "This will put the fire out," he said.
He pushed until the flames were out.

"That's it. The fire's out," said Lugs.
"Well done, Mr Max. You have saved the lab," said Smith.
"That's OK," said Mr Max.

Suddenly an alarm went off!

"That's the rocket," said Smith. "Something must be wrong!"

He ran to the screen and pushed some buttons. The rocket came up on the screen.

"Look! This is inside the rocket. Something really *is* wrong!"

"It will blow up," said Smith.

"I'll fix it," said Mr Max.

"No! Get out of here. It's too late. You can't fix it," said Smith.

"Oh yes, I can. Pass the garlic crisps, Lugs," said Mr Max.

Mr Max ran out of the lab.
The rocket was on the pad.
Sparks were shooting out
of the rocket's nose.
"I've got to get up there
fast," he said. "If this rocket
blows up it will destroy
the lab."

Mr Max ate the garlic crisps fast.
Then he blew into the bag.

He burst the bag with his hands. He spun round and
round. There was a flash. Now he was Mega Max!
"Let's go!" he said.

Mega Max ran across the pad. He hit the button on his sky-pack. He zoomed up. There were steps beside the rocket with a deck at the top. Mega Max landed on the deck. Sparks were shooting out of the rocket's nose.

Back in the lab Smith turned to his screen.

"Who's that by the rocket?" he said.

"It's Mega Max," said Lugs.

"But the rocket's going to blow up!" said Smith.

Mega Max pulled the side of the rocket open. The
nose was full of wires. There were sparks shooting
everywhere.
"Big problem," he said.

Then he pulled out a bag of garlic crisps.
"It's a good job I had two. I always carry an extra
bag," he said.
Lugs saw him eat the crisps. "Not two bags. That's too
many crisps," he said.

Mega Max turned to the sparks. Then he blew hard.

The sparks went out.
"Look! He's done it!" said Smith. "We're all safe!"

"I'm glad that's over. Now I need a cup of Cosmic Cola," said Lugs. He pushed the button on the desk. "Aah!" yelled Smith. "That's not the Cosmic Cola button. That's the rocket button!"
"Oops," said Lugs.

They all ran to the window. Flames and smoke were shooting out of the rocket. It began to move.
It shot up into the sky ... then it began to turn round.
"Look out! It's coming back!" said Smith.

Smith ran to his computer. He pressed the keypad.
The computer was tracking the rocket.

"It's going to hit Mega City. It will blow the city up," he
said.
"We need Mega Max," said Lugs.

"Where is he?" said Smith.

"I'll call him on the Mega Phone," said Lugs.

"Mega Max, come in please. Mega Max, where are you?"

Then the rocket came onto the big screen in the lab.

"Look at that!" said Smith.

"There's a man sitting on the rocket," said Smith.
"It's Mega Max," said Lugs.
"Get off there, Mega Max. That rocket is going to hit the city. It's going to blow up," said Smith.

"Turn it round," said Mega Max.

"I can't," said Smith.

"You will have to do it, sir," said Lugs.

"How can I?" said Mega Max.

"You've had two bags of crisps. You can do it!" said Lugs.

Mega Max looked down at Mega City. It was coming up fast. Past the city was the sea. It was deep blue in the sun.

"I have a plan," he said. He hit the button on his sky-pack.

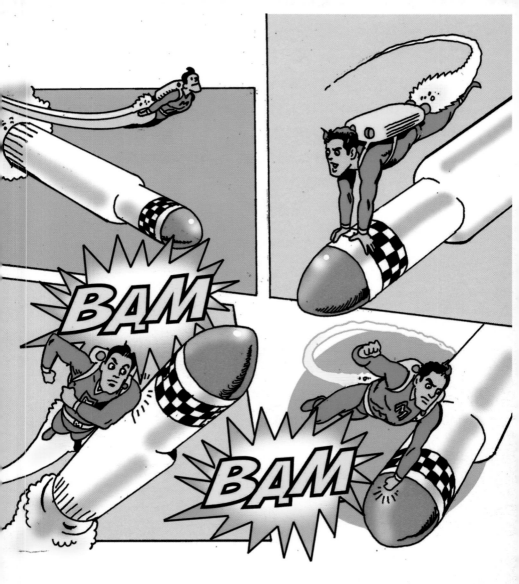

Mega Max jumped off the rocket. He shot up, then dived back down. He flew along by the rocket. Then he hit the rocket hard with his fist. He hit it on the nose.

"What's he doing?" asked Smith.

"He's hitting the rocket. He's trying to turn it," said Lugs.

Mega Max hit the rocket again. Slowly it began to turn. It began to head for the sea.

"He's doing it!" yelled Smith.

The rocket shot over the lab. Mega Max went after it. The rocket slammed into the sea. A big wall of water shot up.

"He did it!" yelled Smith.

Mega Max dived down to the lab.
"You saved the city. Are you OK?" asked Smith.
"Yes, but I'd love a cup of Cosmic Cola, Lugs," said
Mega Max.
"Of course, sir ..." said Lugs, "but this time I'll let Mr
Smith press the button!"